W9-CTS-938

Oakdale S. D. A.
Church School
1501 Magnolia
Oakdale, California

A Walk
by the Seashore

WALLACE KIRKLAND

REILLY & LEE BOOKS · CHICAGO

594.92
Ki

OTHER BOOKS IN THE SERIES:

A Walk in the Fields
A Walk in the Mountains
A Walk by the Pond
A Walk in the Woods

I wish to thank Tom Stack for his encouragement
and his help in filling gaps in my photography files.
Wallace Kirkland

Copyright © 1971 by Wallace Kirkland. All rights reserved.
Published by Reilly & Lee Books, a division of Henry Regnery Company
114 West Illinois Street, Chicago, Illinois 60610
Manufactured in the United States of America
Library of Congress Catalog Card Number: 78-163271

To Parents and Teachers

I was born in Jamaica. Our house stood in a grove of coconut trees on a high cliff overlooking the Caribbean. In my childhood, the sea was ever present, and during storms, when the white-crested breakers crashed against the cliffs, I could feel the house shake. Nightly I was lulled to sleep by the sound of the sea.

Of course, a book such as this is no substitute for the kind of first-hand experience of the ocean that I enjoyed as a child. But I hope that it will serve as an interesting introduction to the myriad forms of life that abound along our coasts.

Parents and teachers using this book can supplement the text in a number of ways. They might, for example, point out how the body structures of the various creatures described are uniquely suited to the kind of life they lead. The effect of the tide upon the life of the shore and the interdependence among its creatures cannot be overemphasized. And, of course, a sympathetic adult can do much to stimulate young readers to further independent study.

As I was assembling the photographs and writing the text for this book, I often found my mind wandering back to my childhood in Jamaica—far removed from the shores of our continent, and yet similar in so many ways. Since then I have walked hundreds of miles along our continental shores—and I hope that my readers will be encouraged to do the same.

Wallace Kirkland

The two great oceans that wash up on our beaches are the Atlantic on the east and the Pacific on the west. As you might guess, the thousands of miles of shores that line our continent are the home of great numbers of creatures. Pretend that we can move from one part of our shoreline to another as fast as we wish. This way we can look at many forms of life that are found along the different seashores that surround our continent.

When the sea rises and moves up on the beaches, we say it is flood tide, or high tide; when the sea falls away from the shore, we say it is ebb tide, or low tide. The tides are caused by gravity — the same force that makes a ball you toss into the air fall back down to earth. The pull of gravity among the sun, moon, and earth makes the surface of the ocean rise and fall twice a day. The tides touch the lives of all the shore animals.

This giant keyhole limpet lives along rocky shores.
The limpet makes a "home" for itself by rubbing
its shell back and forth against a rock until it makes a
groove in the rock that is exactly the same shape
as its shell. During high tide, the limpet moves
among the rocks searching for food. When the tide
begins to ebb, the limpet returns to its groove, pulls
its shell down tight, and clings to the rock. The
limpet's grip is so strong that water does not
leak out from underneath its shell, and air cannot leak
in. Thus the limpet remains safe until the tide
comes back in.

Sea animals with soft bodies and hard, protective shells are called "mollusks." Limpets are mollusks, and so are abalones. Abalones live on rocks near the bottom of the sea and close to shore. In the United States they are found off the California coast, where divers scoop them up to sell as food. Abalone shells are valuable for their linings of mother-of-pearl.

Blue mussels can be found along the Atlantic shore. Their two close-fitting shells help keep them from drying out when the tide is low and give them a special name, "bivalves." The mussel puts out a fluid that sticks to rocks and hardens in water. The animal attaches itself to one spot by putting out several of these "anchor threads." When a mussel wants to move, it breaks the old threads and makes new ones in the direction it wants to go. Then it drags itself along.

Clams, like blue mussels, are bivalves. Clams, which
make their homes along sandy shores, use a
digging "foot" to bury themselves beneath the sand.
You can find hundreds of different clams throughout
the world. The razor clam's foot swells up under
the sand and grips so tightly that if you try
to pull the creature out, its shell will break. The
coquina clam is carried up and down the beach by the
tide waters. It uses its foot to sink out of sight
when danger approaches. In the giant clam you see
here, it is easy to spot the strong muscle that
holds the two parts of the shell closed tight.

The hard little bumps on the topside of the starfish
help protect its soft body. The starfish breathes
through puffy little water sacs, or gills, all over its arms.
Hundreds of tiny tube feet on the underside of the
arms enable the starfish to move.

Clams and other bivalves are a favorite food of the
starfish. It wraps its arms around a shellfish
and pulls until the shell opens just a little. Then
the starfish pushes its stomach out through the small
mouth in the middle of its underside. The starfish
digests its meal outside its body and then pulls its
stomach back inside.

A relative of the starfish is a spiny, gray-green ball
called a sea urchin. Like the starfish, the
sea urchin cannot live long out of water. There is
a small mouth with five teeth at the bottom of
the animal. The urchin grips the rocks with tiny tube
feet and pushes itself forward with its bottom
spines and teeth. As it walks, its teeth scrape small
plants off the rocks for food.

Sea anemones come in
many colors, but the
kind you are most likely
to find along the shore
has a brown body
and whitish tentacles.
This animal is really a
hollow tube with an
opening and tentacles at
the top. When the
anemone is alarmed, it
folds its tentacles into
its mouth and crouches
down. The sea anemone
is flower-shaped when
it feeds and a rubbery
lump when it hides.

The shore is the home of many kinds of worms.
Although most of them hide deep in the sand
or underneath rocks and seaweed, some worms build
tubes for themselves and attach them to rocks or
seaweed. This featherduster worm is about
half an inch long. It fishes with its "feathers"
extended. When it is frightened, it closes up like a fan
and goes down into its tube. It is sometimes
called a fanworm.

The tiny spider crab is about the size of an ant and spends its entire life underwater.

Crabs come in many sizes and shapes. Some have legs that are long and thin, and others have thick, strong legs. All crabs have bodies that are wider than they are long; two eyes on "stalks;" and ten jointed legs. The crab's body is inside its skeleton — instead of on the outside, as our bodies are. When a crab grows too big for its skeleton, the old shell splits open, and the crab steps out. After a while, a new skeleton hardens. This kind of growth is called "molting."

The sand crab scrambles about on the beach at low tide looking for food.

The barnacle, like the limpet, is well known for its
strong grip. The young barnacle looks something like
a crab and swims freely through the water.
As it grows older, its shape changes several times.
The adult barnacle attaches itself to a rock —
or anything else that's solid — forms a tough shell for
protection, and usually stays in that spot for the
rest of its life. Adult barnacles, like their crab
relatives, grow by molting.

The lobster, like the crab, has a hard skeleton on the outside of its body and five pairs of legs. Its body is longer and thinner than the crab's, and since it lives far out from the shore, you are not likely to see it — except in a restaurant! The lobster's two claws are different. One acts like a scissors, and the other like a pair of pliers. On a lobster's tail there are a number of small paddles called "swimmerets." The swimmerets help the lobster move forward, and they also hold the eggs after they have been laid. By snapping its tail quickly underneath its body, the lobster can dart backward.

Sponges have no legs or arms, no eyes or mouth.
But they, too, are living animals. Water sweeps
through hundreds of tiny holes to the inside layers,
where bits of food carried in the water are swallowed.
Then the water is pushed out again. Sponges
that live close to a rocky shore spread out low and
thin so that the waves washing over them will not
break off pieces. Tall sponges, such as the ones you
see here, grow farther offshore, where the
water is deeper and quieter. Some deep-water sponges
make supporting structures for their bodies out
of a substance called "spongin." The "skeletons" of
these animals are used as bath sponges.

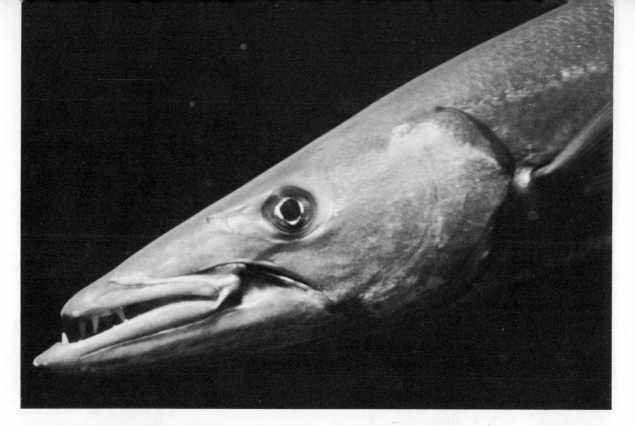

The ocean waters, of course, are the home of
thousands of different fish. The barracuda is one of
the most fierce. It grows from six to eight feet long.
It preys on smaller fish, and it will attack human
swimmers.

The stingray is a large, flat fish with a long, flexible
tail. It swims along the sea bottom with a
bat-like motion. Stingrays eat small sea animals,
including shellfish. They also "scavenge," or feed on
dead matter. There are sharp spines along the
stingray's tail. When the fish is disturbed, it swings
its tail upward and sideways and can give a swimmer
a painful wound.

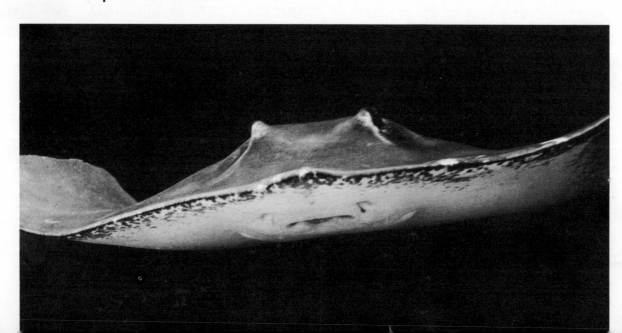

The shark is another dangerous fish that sometimes comes close to the shore. You should avoid all three of these fishes and warn other swimmers if you spot one of them near the beach.

Sea lions like to play games, and on the West Coast,
at the cliff rocks near San Francisco, you can
watch them romp and play.

The birds found along a shore get their food from the sea. The birds nest in the trees or in the sea cliffs, dunes, and marshes near the shore. There they hatch their young and feed them — either with food washed up on shore by the tide or with sea life caught from the waters.

The most common birds found along the shore are
the seagulls. Gulls eat mussels, clams, dead fish,
and other food that washes up on the beach. Often
you can see flocks of gulls waiting patiently for
the tide to go out so they can feed.

Egrets wade near the shore and in pools left by
the tide, searching for snails and small fish. Years ago,
the tail feathers of egrets were much sought after
for use in women's hats, and the number of these
birds was greatly reduced. Now, however, egrets are
protected by law.

The pelican is the largest of the web-footed birds.
It weighs up to sixteen pounds and has a wingspread
of from eight to twelve feet. Pelicans band
together in large groups, or "colonies." The
enormous pouches attached to their lower beaks can
store quarts of small fish, which the pelicans eat
at their leisure or carry to their young.

Spoonbills wade in the tide pools on their long legs and strain food from the water with their beaks.

The anhinga is sometimes called the water turkey.
The young birds are brownish, and the adults
are black with long, snake-like necks and long tails.
Anhingas can swim underwater faster than the
fish they feed upon.

The black-bellied plover is a plump wader, with a bill
that looks like a pigeon's. It feeds chiefly on
small sea creatures, and it migrates as far as 2,000
miles every year.

The frigate, or man-o'-war, bird is unsurpassed in
powers of flight. It is known as the swiftest bird to
sweep the seas. Most sea birds have special glands
that waterproof their feathers with oil. The frigate
bird does not have these glands, so it never lands
on the water. Instead it uses its long, hooked bill
to attack other birds and rob them of their fish catches.

The female frigate bird has pink feet; the male's
feet are black. During the mating sason, the
male inflates a bright patch underneath his bill.

More than two-thirds of the earth's surface—
140 million square miles—is covered by oceans. When
you walk by the seashore, you can use all your
senses to learn about the life of the sea. Feel the
sand tickling your feet, taste the salt of
the water, listen to the sound of the waves and the
gulls, smell the sea air, watch a sand crab
scurry across the beach. In these pages we have
looked at only a few of the hundreds of creatures that
make their homes near the ocean. But if you
visit the shore yourself and sit quietly near a tide pool
or a spot that is safe at high tide, you are certain to
learn about many more creatures—including yourself.

Oakdale S. D. A.
Church School
1501 Magnolia
Oakdale, California